Prepared by the Department of the Environ
Ancient Monuments and Historic Buildings

Border Warfa

A HISTORY OF CONFLICT ON
THE ANGLO-SCOTTISH BORDER

ANTHONY TUCK MA, PhD

*Master of Collingwood College and Honorary Lecturer in History,
University of Durham*

LONDON: HER MAJESTY'S STATIONERY OFFICE

Caerlaverock Castle, Dumfriesshire, as it might have appeared in
the fifteenth century, from a drawing by Alan Sorrell

ISBN 0 11 670817 4

Border Warfare

For nearly two thousand years the land between the Tyne–Solway gap and the Forth–Clyde isthmus has been a frontier region between the peoples occupying the northern and the southern parts of the island of Britain. The underlying reason for this is the region's physical geography, and in particular the shortness of the main routes from east to west. From the Solway to the mouth of the Tyne the distance is about 70 miles (113km); the route from the Solway to the mouth of the Esk at Inveresk is slightly shorter, and the route across central Scotland from the Firth of Forth to the Firth of Clyde is only about 40 miles (64km). The present Anglo-Scottish border, on the Tweed–Cheviot–Solway line, is much the longest of the various east–west routes in the region, being about 90 miles (145km) in length.

The Romans were the first to form a defined frontier in this region of Britain. Agricola, on his advance north in AD80, established a temporary frontier on the Forth–Clyde line as a preliminary to a further advance into the highlands, which came in AD83. But the position he established in the highlands could not be held, and early in the second century the Romans retreated to the Tyne–Solway line. One of Agricola's achievements did however, endure: he laid down the basic network of communications which determined movement in the region until the eighteenth century. He established two principal north–south routes: a western route from Carlisle via Lockerbie, Crawford and Biggar to Edinburgh; and an eastern route, Dere Street, from Corbridge via High Rochester, Newstead and Dalkeith to Edinburgh. A subsidiary route, the Devil's Causeway, ran north from Corbridge to Berwick-upon-Tweed, but the coastal route from Berwick to Edinburgh remained of only local importance until the nineteenth century.

In AD121 the Emperor Hadrian came to Britain and inspected the Tyne–Solway frontier. He had recently established a continuous barrier along the Rhine in Germany, and with this in mind he decided to mark the frontier of Roman Britain with a continuous wall from Newcastle upon Tyne (later from Wallsend) to Bowness-on-Solway, a distance of 68 miles (100km). The wall itself was complemented by a series of outpost forts to the north, but the essential concept which Hadrian introduced was that of a linear, fortified, and regularly patrolled frontier. Hadrian's Wall did not, however, remain the frontier for long. In campaigns between 139 and 142, Lollius Urbicus, the governor of Britain, reoccupied the land between the Wall and the Forth–Clyde isthmus, and he applied to the new frontier the same principles of demarcation and defence that Hadrian had laid down. Thus a second Roman wall, the Antonine Wall, was built from Carriden in the east

to Old Kilpatrick in the west, a distance of 37 miles (60km). This wall was abandoned briefly in *c*155, reoccupied shortly afterwards and held until *c*163, and then finally abandoned in favour of the Tyne–Solway line. In 205–08 the Emperor Severus ordered such a thoroughgoing reconstruction of Hadrian's Wall that it was for long believed that he had been its original builder.

The wall was abandoned in 410, together with the rest of Roman Britain, and a number of Romano-British successor states emerged both in the Romanised lands south of the wall and in the areas under Roman military protection and military surveillance to the north. There is no evidence that the wall was of any significance as a frontier in the tangled and obscure history of the successor states. More important than the fate of the Roman frontier was the settlement in the east of new peoples with whom the political and cultural future was to lie—the Angles. Anglo-Saxon tradition preserved the memory of the seizure of Bamburgh rock by Ida in AD547, and this tradition is borne out by place-name evidence which suggests Anglian

4

settlement on some of the better land between the Forth and the Tyne in the sixth and seventh centuries. These settlers gave an Anglian imprint to what is now south-east Scotland as well as to Northumbria; while in the west Celtic peoples held their own for a time, and thus a linguistic (and for some while a cultural and religious) frontier ran north–south through the region, leaving the east coast in the hands of the initially pagan Anglian settlers. But the pirate stronghold at Bamburgh developed rapidly, by war and marriage, into a kingdom (Bernicia) which controlled not only Northumberland and Lothian but also much of the rest of the region. It included Cumbria and Galloway and, at the time of its greatest extent, it reached as far as Ayrshire in the north-west. Edinburgh was an Anglian stronghold, and Glasgow and Dumbarton were on the fringes of Anglian power. In the eighth century Bernicia was submerged in an uneasy union with another Anglian kingdom, Deira, centred on York, and at the height of its power, in the age of Bede (died 735) this united kingdom of Northumbria dominated not only the north but the whole of Britain. A brilliant culture developed in Northumbria in this period, epitomised by the Lindisfarne Gospels, the Ruthwell and Bewcastle crosses, and the work of Bede. This culture was common to what is now northern England and southern Scotland. The northern frontier of the kingdom lay on the Forth–Clyde line, and the Tyne–Solway and Tweed–Solway lines were of no more than minor administrative importance. The Anglian period imposed a cultural, linguistic and religious homogeneity on the region which it was never entirely to lose.

However, the Anglian hegemony, like the Roman, was disrupted by internal disorder and external attack. The external attack came from the Vikings, who raided the east coast in the late eighth and ninth centuries from Norway and Denmark, and who attacked the west coast a little later from their settlements in Ireland. The raids terrified the inhabitants of eastern Northumbria, but did not lead to any extensive settlement in Northumberland or Lothian. The Anglian character of these regions was not greatly modified, in contrast to the lands further south in the 'Danelaw'. In the west, however, Viking settlement was extensive both in Cumbria and in Galloway, as place names ending in -by and -bie suggest. Thus a linguistic and cultural frontier running north to south through the region was re-created after its momentary effacement under Anglian rule. Galloway and Cumbria were held together by common Norse-Celtic ties, while Northumberland and Lothian shared a common Englishness. The Vikings, however, did not seek to establish a unitary state in the north-west, and they were prepared, together with the English of the east, to accept the overlordship in the tenth century of the kings of Wessex, who were rapidly becoming kings of all England.

The writ of these kings ran nominally as far as Edinburgh in the east and Strathclyde in the west. But they could not easily control these regions in the face of pressure from a newly powerful Scottish kingdom born of the union in 843 of the Picts and the Scots of Dalriada (roughly modern Argyll). In 945 Edmund of England granted Strathclyde, which probably included Cumbria, to the Scottish king, though the extent and character of the Scottish king's authority in Cumbria remains uncertain. In the east, Edinburgh passed into the hands of the Scots about 960, and in 975 Edgar of England ceremonially handed Lothian over to Kenneth, king of Scots. The cession of Lothian was confirmed by the Scottish victory at the battle of Carham, *c*1016. This contraction of English power brought the Anglo-Scottish border to its present line in the east (though Berwick, of course, was in Scotland) and to the Rere Cross on Stainmore (near Bowes, Yorks.) in the west.

In what remained of Northumbria, the authority of the last Anglo-Saxon kings and of William the Conqueror was delegated to an earl, who was sometimes a member of the ancient ruling house of Bamburgh. In the face of this loose control by the kings of England, it is not surprising that the Scottish kings tried to involve themselves in Northumbrian affairs by marrying into the family of the earls in the early eleventh century, and by offering shelter to members of the Northumbrian aristocracy, especially after 1066. Their ultimate object was to push the border further south, to the Tyne, the Tees, or even the Ribble.

The Norman conquest of England made little difference at first to the aspirations of the Scottish kings; but it gradually modified the social structure of both northern England and southern and eastern Scotland, and it almost certainly brought about important innovations in the defence of the border. We do not know how the Anglo-Saxons defended their frontier with the Scots. They clearly did not think of it as a continuous line to be systematically patrolled, as the Romans did. Yet so far no Anglo-Saxon material has come to light from any of the major medieval fortress sites on either side of the border, and the little we know about the campaigns of the early eleventh century suggests that there were no important fortified strong points along the line of the border. The Normans, however, revolutionised both military tactics and defensive methods. Norman lords received land in Northumberland in the late 1080s and 1090s; they came to Cumberland after 1092, when

William II led an expedition to Carlisle, drove out the local ruler and established the border on its present line in the west (though the parish of Kirkandrews lay in Scotland). In the twelfth century, Norman lords began to penetrate southern Scotland. The Normans did not seek to establish a linear, defined frontier between England and Scotland. To them the castle was the key to defence, and the highly mobile cavalry force dominated warfare in the field. On the border, therefore, the Normans built castles to command the land they held and to control and defend the principal routes across the border. The pattern of fortifications established by the Normans thus bears some relation to the network of communications laid down by Agricola.

The earliest castles were mottes, some of which had baileys as well. Excellent examples remain at Elsdon in Northumberland (owned by the Umfraville family) and at Liddel Strength in Cumbria (held by Turgis Brundis). Elsdon commands the Dere Street route across the border, and Liddel Strength lies close to the Roman fort of Netherby, on the road north from Carlisle. Such fortresses served to hold the border in the reigns of the first three Norman kings. In the reign of Stephen, however, David I of Scotland, ostensibly upholding the cause of Matilda, Stephen's rival for the English throne, invaded northern England. He was defeated at the Battle of the Standard, near Northallerton in 1139, but even so Stephen acquiesced in his control of northern England as far as the Tees in the east and the Ribble in the west. These areas became effectively part of the Scottish realm, even though David's son Henry held the earldom of Northumberland as a fief of the English crown. David himself held his court at both Newcastle and Carlisle, and Carlisle seems to have been one of his favourite residences. He died there in 1153.

The return of strong government in England under Henry II (1154–89) meant that the Scots would come under pressure to abandon their occupation of northern England, and in 1157 Malcolm IV formally relinquished the region to Henry. In a final attempt to carry the frontier south to the Tyne and claim the earldom of Northumberland, Malcolm's successor William I 'The Lion' (1165–1214) invaded Northumberland, but was captured in a skirmish at Alnwick in 1173. William's capture and the Treaty of Falaise which followed it ended one phase of Anglo-Scottish relations. The Scots did not formally renounce their claim to Northumberland until 1237, but it became clear by the beginning of the thirteenth century that Scottish rule was not going to extend south of the Tweed–Solway line.

None the less, Henry II and his successors could not afford to abandon the fortresses along the border. The castle was still the key to defence, and the region shared fully in the developments in the technique of fortification which took place in the second half of the twelfth century. The earliest castles at strongpoints such as Carlisle, Norham, Elsdon, and Berwick were in all probability built of wood and surrounded by wooden palisades rather than stone walls. But in the twelfth century the growing wealth and power of the kings and the greatest of the nobles, such as the Bishop of Durham, made it possible for them to use stone, a much more expensive material, in their fortresses. The stone keep of Richmond castle, which commands the Roman road from Cumbria to Yorkshire, was built between 1150 and 1180. The keep of the Bishop of Durham's castle at Norham, which guards an important ford over the Tweed, was built about the same time, as were the keeps of the royal castles of Carlisle and Newcastle. In all these castles the keep is the key building. It is square in plan and massive in construction; a citadel to be defended even if the stone curtain wall is breached.

In the century after the Treaty of Falaise the border region enjoyed peace and prosperity. Berwick became one of the largest and wealthiest burghs in Scotland. It had a large mercantile community engaged in the export trade in wool, and the kings had their most important mint there. A contemporary chronicler described Berwick as 'A second Alexandria, whose riches was the sea and the water was its walls.' Unlike Newcastle and Carlisle, Berwick was not walled in the thirteenth century. The castle stood adjacent to the town but the town was defended merely by a stockade and a ditch.

In this period, too, the English monarchy developed its administrative and financial resources, so that it was able in the next phase of Anglo-Scottish conflict to mobilise large armies and supply trains, and construct new fortresses, in an effort to assert mastery not just over a frontier region but over the whole of Scotland.

Taking advantage of a dispute over the succession to the Scottish throne after the death in 1290 of Queen Margaret, the 'Maid of Norway', Edward I of England (1272–1307) attempted to impose his overlordship on Scotland.

He attempted first of all to rule through John Balliol (1292–96), his vassal king of Scots, and then, when Balliol was goaded into defiance, he sought to rule the country directly and to destroy or remove the symbols of the Scottish monarchy, the great seal, the regalia, and the Stone of Scone. In the space of a few years, from 1292 to 1296, the cordial relations that had existed between two kingdoms similar in language, culture, and political organisation became transformed into a hostility that was to last for three hundred years.

On the outbreak of open war between the two kingdoms in 1296, Edward's first target was Berwick. On 30 March he took the town by storm and the inhabitants were put to the sword. Edward now intended the town to form a bastion of English authority in Scotland and to serve as a supply base for his troops. The castle was substantially rebuilt, and the town itself received a stone wall, of which the White Wall is a survival. Elsewhere in Scotland, however, Edward's building was on a limited scale and cannot be compared with his work in North Wales. English forces occupied many existing castles in the Lowlands, some of which—e.g. Linlithgow—Edward strengthened with earth and timber outworks. But it appears that he did not build any new castles; existing fortresses served his purpose well enough, and he probably hoped that the Scots would eventually acquiesce in English rule, making a permanent English presence in strength unnecessary.

In the event, however, Edward failed both to subdue Scotland by military force and to persuade the Scots to accept a political settlement in which ultimate control lay with the English king. The deposition of Balliol and such brutalities as the massacre at Berwick served only to stiffen Scottish resistance and to call into existence a more precise national sentiment than had existed before. Scottish resistance was led first by William Wallace, who inflicted a defeat on the English, in the absence of Edward, at Stirling Bridge in September 1297. This victory invited retaliation from Edward. The following year he marched north at the head of his army and won a notable victory at Falkirk. Even this victory, however, did not give him mastery of Scotland. The long supply lines, the cost of maintaining an army in Scotland, the nature of the Scottish terrain, and the domestic problems to which war taxation gave rise, made permanent domination of the country impossible.

With the accession to the English throne of the feeble and incompetent Edward II (1307–27), the balance of advantage in the war swung in favour of the Scots. Scottish resistance found a new leader in Robert Bruce, who rose against Edward in 1306 and soon gathered much support. Many castles fell to him, though Berwick withstood a siege in 1312, and Stirling held out for the English. It was to relieve Stirling Castle that Edward II embarked upon the campaign that led to his ignominious defeat at the Battle of Bannockburn on 24 June 1314. In this battle the English cavalry dashed itself to pieces on the Scottish schiltrons, hedgehog-like formations of spearmen, and Edward failed to use his longbowmen to break up the schiltrons. Bannockburn was the fourth battle in twenty years in which the infantry had played a decisive part, and it was clear that the domination of battle by the feudal cavalry was at an end. At Stirling Bridge Wallace had successfully used schiltrons; at Falkirk Edward I, building on his Welsh experiences, had used longbowmen with devastating effect against the Scottish schiltrons; and in 1302 the French cavalry had been routed by the pikemen of the Flemish weaving cities at the Battle of Courtrai. The future, however, was to lie with the longbow rather than with the schiltrons, and Edward III's use of his longbowmen was to bring him victory against the Scots at Halidon Hill in 1333 and against the French at Crecy and Poitiers.

After Bannockburn the Scots took the offensive against northern England. Since 1296 the north had suffered the occasional Scottish raid, but now the Scots penetrated deeply into the northern counties, forcing the local communities to purchase immunity and burning and looting if they failed to do so. They used the main lines of communication, and fell upon the easily accessible and wealthy agrarian communities. The Roman road pattern helped to determine the direction of the raids, and the remoter upland regions escaped comparatively lightly. Bruce also turned his attention to Berwick and Carlisle. Carlisle withstood a siege in 1315, when the town was ably defended by Sir Andrew Harcla, but Berwick fell to Bruce in 1318 and an English counter-attack failed in the following year. Berwick now remained in Scottish hands until after Halidon Hill in 1333.

Under the Treaty of Edinburgh, 1328, the English acknowledged Scottish independence. But the war was resumed in 1332 when a group of English lords who had lost land in Scotland succeeded for a time in putting a puppet king, Edward Balliol (1332–36), on the Scottish throne and driving out Bruce's son and heir David II (1329–71). Once again the English won pitched battles, such as Dupplin Moor in 1332 and Halidon Hill in 1333, but once again victory in the field did not give them mastery of the country. During his brief reign, however, Edward Balliol handed over much of southern Scotland to Edward III. For a few years the border ran from the Cree to the Avon, and the north of England felt momentarily secure. Berwick was to be

A vicar's pele at Corbridge, Northumberland

the administrative headquarters of English-occupied Scotland, and the English hastily repaired the principal fortresses in the newly occupied territory. But Edward III's preoccupation with the French war after 1337 allowed the Scots to begin the recovery of their lost lands, and to help their French ally by tying down English forces north of the border. Over the next twenty years the English were gradually driven back to the present border line, so that by 1357 they held little more than a chain of fortresses on the Scottish side: Lochmaben, Jedburgh, Roxburgh, Fast Castle, and Berwick.

In this phase of the war the Scottish border counties suffered more than the English; Scottish raids into England were less frequent than they had been in the years after Bannockburn, but on both sides of the border men became resigned to unending conflict, and all those who could afford to do so built themselves fortified dwellings. Security was the overriding consideration in the architecture of the period. Houses built without defences on a more peaceful age, such as Langley or Featherstone, were hastily fortified; church towers were built or rebuilt with an eye to defence, and some vicars built themselves fortified dwellings, the so-called vicars' peles. For lesser men, the

13

characteristic form of fortified dwelling was the pele tower or tower house, a rectangular or square building often protected with a palisade (Latin *pilum* from which the term pele is derived). The great lords built themselves massive fortifications such as the grim castle of Hermitage in Liddesdale or the more luxurious Warkworth Castle. But how ever small or how ever opulent, each building had to be designed primarily to resist attack. The peasantry, on the other hand, who could not afford stone towers or peles, had little alternative but to accept raids as another hazard of life, though in 1323 the inhabitants of Bamburgh apparently dismantled the timber frames of their houses at the approach of the Scots and took them into the castle.

On the Scottish side of the border the principal fortresses were slighted when they were recaptured by the Scots, so as to deny them to the English in any future invasion. This explains why so little survives of so important a fortress as Roxburgh. Under English occupation, however, Berwick retained its defences, and the town achieved a certain hazardous prosperity and importance as the principal administrative, supply and garrison centre for English-occupied Scotland. This area was eventually reduced to the town itself and its immediate hinterland, but it retained an anomalous status as part of neither country until 1888. The recovery of Berwick was a paramount goal of Scottish policy, and was achieved briefly in 1355, 1384, and, in complicity with the Earl of Northumberland, in 1405. It passed into Scottish hands again in 1461, but its recapture by the English in 1482 proved final.

In southern England in the late fourteenth century, fortresses such as Cooling Castle and the West Gate of Canterbury were adapted for firearms; and the castle of Ravenscraig, Fife, built *c*1460 for Mary of Guelders, James II's queen, shows the very latest French techniques of fortification being employed. On the Anglo-Scottish border, however, there is evidence only at Threave Castle of the construction of an artillery fortification. None the less, firearms were used in border warfare in the later Middle Ages. Edward III had guns with him on his Weardale campaign in 1327, and guns were used at the siege of Berwick in 1333. These early guns may have resembled the illustration in the Millemete MS, which shows a gun shaped like a vase and firing a projectile resembling a cross-bow bolt. From about 1360 much bigger guns, bombards, made of cast iron, appear. James II was killed by a bombard at the siege of Roxburgh in 1460, but despite the size and the noise of the bombards it is unlikely that they played a decisive part in the outcome of any siege or battle in Britain in the fifteenth century. Warfare on

the border was conservative in its methods and techniques in the later Middle Ages. A pattern of raid and counter-raid, punctuated by occasional full-scale expeditions culminating in pitched battles such as Neville's Cross, Otterburn, and Homildon Hill, persisted throughout the fourteenth and fifteenth centuries. The warfare between the two countries encouraged lawlessness and feuding between landowners great and small on either side of the border, and in such raids and feuds considerations of honour and vengeance often played a larger part than political issues.

In the later stages of the Wars of the Roses in England, Margaret of Anjou used Scotland and certain castles in Northumberland as a Lancastrian base; but with the return of more settled government under the Yorkists and early Tudors the north was brought more firmly under central control, and

Henry VII sought a settlement with James IV of Scotland. In 1502 the two countries signed a treaty of peace, and Henry's daughter Margaret was married to James. From this marriage James VI derived his title to the English throne in 1603.

This peace did not long endure. Henry VIII's accession to the Holy League against France revived the Franco-Scottish alliance, and James IV invaded England in 1513, to be disastrously defeated at Flodden. The overwhelming English victory at Flodden was won by foot soldiers armed with pikes. In this sense, it was one of the last 'medieval' battles to be fought in Britain, for although James IV brought his train of seven culverins, the 'Seven Sisters,' they did not play a decisive part in the battle. On the Continent, however, important developments were taking place in the use of artillery. Guns became smaller, and there was some attempt to standardise them according to calibre. Brass came to be used in their manufacture, thus reducing the risk of fracture. In France especially, royal artillery was used to much greater effect than before, and to combat the increasing effectiveness of cannon, continental engineers devised new forms of fortification. They advocated the adoption of lower but much thicker masonry walls that would absorb the impact of cannon balls, and the building of round bastions and gun emplacements which would provide defensive fire from the fortress. Albrecht Dürer published a treatise on fortification in 1527 in which he advocated the adoption of the circular bastioned fortress.

In the fifteenth and early sixteenth centuries, Scotland was more advanced than England in military architecture. The artillery fortification at Threave dates from the 1450s, and Ravenscraig Castle, built in the 1460s, was designed to be defended against an artillery attack. The front of the castle is an oblong block flanked by semi-circular towers of massive masonry with widely splayed gun loops giving a commanding field of fire across the main entrance. These developments were not followed up, but about 1520 a fort was constructed at Dunbar in accordance with latest Continental ideas. This fort was polygonal on plan and consisted of thick masonry walls with gun ports. England, on the other hand, had nothing to compare with Threave, Ravenscraig, or Dunbar. In 1509 part of Norham Castle was equipped with gun ports, but Continental ideas had little impact in England until the 1530s, when Henry VIII placed England's defences in a state of readiness in the face of an invasion threat following his break with Rome. Henry took a personal interest in artillery and in the latest techniques of fortification. He brought Flemish gun founders to England, and in the 1530s a Bohemian

engineer, Stefan von Haschenperg, entered his service. Haschenperg may have had some responsibility for the design and construction of the group of fortresses built to defend the south coast in the 1530s: they are circular forts, with thick masonry walls and gunports. In 1541 Haschenperg was placed in charge of works at Carlisle, and his signed plans for the fortifications there survive. He constructed the half-moon battery, covering the gate leading into the inner ward of the castle, and he began work on the citadel. The work at Carlisle has clear affinities with the South Coast work.

At Berwick in the 1530s the new work was less ambitious. Small gun-towers were added at points on the existing medieval fortifications, and in 1532 work began on Lord's Mount, a large circular tower at the north-east angle of the town wall. This tower had thick masonry walls; it was two storeys in height, the lower provided with gun ports. These new fortifications

17

Contemporary drawing of the Battle of Pinkie, 1547.
The Scots, on the right, are faced by Hertford's forces and are flanked
by English cannon mounted on ships in the Firth of Forth

at Berwick and Carlisle, however, were never put to a serious test. The English invaded Scotland but were defeated at Haddon Rigg in 1542 and the Scottish counter-invasion ended in disaster at Solway Moss later the same year.

In the later 1540s it became the policy of Henry VIII, and after his death in 1547 the policy of the English council, to seek the hand of the infant Mary Queen of Scots for the Prince of Wales, later Edward VI. In two destructive campaigns in 1544–45, known as the 'rough wooing', the Earl of Hertford tried unsuccessfully to force the Scots to agree to the marriage. In pursuit of the same policy, Hertford, now Duke of Somerset, invaded Scotland in 1547 and routed the Scots at Pinkie. Pinkie was the first battle in Britain to be won by fire power, and Somerset used cannon mounted on ships off Musselburgh as well as land-based artillery. After Pinkie, Somerset imposed a military occupation on part of southern Scotland, which lasted until 1550.

At this time the English adopted new ideas on artillery fortification which were derived from Italy. Italian engineers developed two new principles: in

18

the walls of fortifications solid masonry was replaced by earth, faced and held together with masonry; and the round bastion was replaced by the angle bastion with sunken flankers to provide covering fire along the sides of a fortification. When the English took Boulogne in 1544 they fortified it in accordance with these new principles, and when Somerset built forts at Eyemouth, Lauder, Haddington and Dunglass, and refortified Roxburgh, to house his garrisons in southern Scotland, he employed engineers who had had experience at Boulogne. These Scottish forts were masonry reinforced earthworks with angle bastions. At Berwick meanwhile work had begun in the north east of the town on the construction of a square earthwork citadel with angle bastions, and further south at Tynemouth a bastioned fortification on 'Italian' lines was added to the medieval castle.

Mary Queen of Scots was betrothed to the Dauphin, later Francis II of France, in 1548, and in the 1550s French influence was predominant at the Scottish court. At the end of Mary Tudor's reign the threat of invasion compelled the English government to reconsider the defence of the border. Berwick's adaptation to artillery fortification had taken place piecemeal over the previous twenty years; it had no complete system of defence and was still vulnerable to artillery attack. Accordingly in 1558 Mary sent Sir Richard Lee to Berwick to plan and construct a full-scale bastioned defence system for the town. The bastions were to be of the angle type, with sunken flankers, constructed of earth and faced and reinforced with masonry. Lee's plan was never fully implemented. Work on the bastions was stopped in 1569, and the medieval wall remained the town's only defence on the south and south-east sides.

The works at Berwick came to an end because the danger from Scotland had greatly diminished. The rising of the 'Lords of the Congregation' in 1559 aimed not only at bringing about a Protestant reformation in religion but also ridding Scotland of French influence. The Protestant party in Scotland sought the help of Elizabeth of England; an Anglo-Scottish army besieged the French garrison in Leith; and on 6 July 1559, under the Treaty of Edinburgh, the French left Scotland. But in 1561 Mary Queen of Scots returned to Scotland from France, and as long as she remained Queen there was a possibility of a revival of Catholic, pro-French influence in Scotland, and consequently danger to England. In Catholic eyes, Mary was the rightful Queen of England after the Pope's excommunication of Elizabeth. However, Mary's struggle to assert her personal authority failed. In 1567 she was forced to abdicate in favour of her infant son James VI, and although in the following

The Elizabethan curtain walls and bastions forming the ramparts fortifying Berwick-upon-Tweed, as seen from the air

year she escaped from imprisonment in Loch Leven Castle she was defeated at Langside and fled to England. Mary's flight, and the firmer establishment of Protestant rule in Scotland, greatly diminished the threat of invasion from Scotland. Relations between the two countries rapidly improved, and James VI succeeded peacefully to the English throne in 1603.

The hostility between England and Scotland in the sixteenth century, however, allowed disorder and lawlessness to flourish in the border areas, and this was not easily suppressed. The Debateable Land, a district in dispute between the two realms and consequently a notorious haunt of criminals, was partitioned by agreement in 1552, but the governments of both countries found it hard to impose order and in times of war found disorder and raiding a positive advantage. Men still, therefore, had to build for defence and protection. On the English side of the border the bastle-house, a fortified farm house, made its appearance, while in Scotland the tower-house remained the favourite fortified dwelling, often protected by a stone enclosing wall

*Greenknowe Tower, Berwickshire, a sixteenth-century
tower-house built to an L-shaped plan*

or *barmkin*. Some of the more important towers and castles in Scotland were equipped with gun-ports, a development which was very rare in England and which reflects the greater importance of private fortresses in the Scottish border country. In this region the crown exercised its authority indirectly through the great families, and the gap between the resources of the crown and the resources of the subject was much less than in England. On both sides of the border, however, the possession of substantial artillery tended to be a royal monopoly, and the masonry and earthwork artillery fortifications were constructed under royal aegis. No private individual could afford to protect himself in this way.

Despite the union of the crowns in 1603, men were only gradually weaned from their habits of raiding and feuding, and bastles and tower-houses were still being built in the early seventeenth century. Berwick remained a frontier town of great importance. Its defences were strengthened after Charles I's religious policy provoked rebellion in Scotland in 1638. In the early stages of the English civil war the town accepted a Scottish garrison, and proposals were made, though successfully resisted, to slight the fortifications. Under Cromwell an English force garrisoned the town and earthwork parapets and gun platforms were constructed on the ramparts, giving them broadly the appearance they have today. A garrison was retained at Berwick throughout the eighteenth century, and in 1721 it took possession of the newly constructed Ravensdowne Barracks.

These developments, however, constitute little more than a postscript to the history of border warfare and of Berwick's part in that warfare. The Scottish reformation and the union of the crowns transformed the relationship between England and Scotland. The border region became the 'middle shires' of James VI and I's kingdom, and Berwick's bastions were never tested in a major siege. They survive, however, as a visible reminder of the last stage in the evolution of the art of fortification on the border, evolution stimulated by three hundred years of hostility between the two kingdoms.

Further Reading

G. W. S. BARROW. *Robert Bruce.* London, 1965.

H. M. COLVIN, ed. *The History of the King's Works*, 2 vols. London, 1963.

W. C. DICKINSON. *Scotland from the Earliest Times to 1603.* Edinburgh, 1961.

G. DONALDSON. *Scotland: James V–James VII.* Edinburgh, 1965.

I. MacIVOR, 1965. The Elizabethan Fortifications of Berwick upon Tweed, *The Antiquaries Journal* XLV: 65–96.

I. MacIVOR. *The Fortifications of Berwick-upon-Tweed.* London, 1967.

SIR CHARLES OMAN. *A History of the Art of War in the Middle Ages*, 2 vols. London, 1924.

SIR CHARLES OMAN. *A History of the Art of War in the 16th Century.* London, 1937.

B. H. ST. J. O'NEILL. *Castles and Cannon.* Oxford, 1960.

Brief accounts of some of the English buildings described in this Handbook or illustrated in the exhibition can be found in volumes in the Buildings of England series edited by N. Pevsner and published by Penguin: *Cumberland and Westmorland* (1967) and *Northumberland* (1957).

Longer descriptions of some of the buildings in Scotland can be found in the inventories of the Royal Commission on the Ancient and Historical Monuments of Scotland for Berwickshire, Dumfries and Roxburgh.

ACKNOWLEDGEMENTS

Grateful acknowledgement is made to Professor McCord of the University of Newcastle upon Tyne for the aerial photograph of Elsdon Castle reproduced on page 7; to the Bodleian Library, Oxford for the manuscript drawing of the Battle of Pinkie (page 18); to the Royal Commission on Ancient Monuments in Scotland for the photograph of Greenhowe Tower (page 21); to John Dewar Studios for the aerial view of Berwick-upon-Tweed (page 20); and to the Scottish Office for photographs of Hermitage Castle (page 13) and the Mons Meg bombard (page 15). The remaining photographs are by the Department of the Environment, who also hold the copyright of the Alan Sorrell drawings on pages 2 and 4.

Printed in Scotland by Her Majesty's Stationery Office at HMSO Press, Edinburgh
Dd 597129 K48 11/79 (15887)